W9-AUS-230

10/02

22.50

Bridges

Nicola Baxter

FRANKLIN WATTS
A Division of Grolier Publishing
NEW YORK • LONDON • HONG KONG • SYDNEY
DANBURY, CONNECTICUT

Cover: Arcaid; AKG (inset)
Interior Pictures:
Illustrations: Peter Bull: 4-5, 11, 17, 18, 22, 26, 28;
Sarah John: 7, 12, 23; Carolyn Scrace: 8, 13, 19, 27.
Photography: AKG: 8, 14 (bottom); Arcaid: 24 (top);
Associated Press: 23; Axion: 28; Sylvia Cordaiy: 5, 19;
Ecoscene: 7, 15, 26 (bottom); David Noble: 4, 10, 20
(bottom); Photodisc: 6 (both), 9, 11, 16, 25 (bottom), 29
(top); Science Photo Library: 29 (bottom); Skyscan: 5, 14,
21 (top); Travel Ink 10 (top), 24.

Series editor: Anderley Moore
Editor: Enid Fisher
Series designer: John Christopher, WHITE DESIGN
Picture research: Sue Mennell
Illustrators: Peter Bull; Sarah John; Carolyn Scrace

First published in 2000 by
Franklin Watts
96 Leonard Street
London
EC2A 4XD

First American edition 2000 by Franklin Watts
A Division of Grolier Publishing
90 Sherman Turnpike
Danbury, CT 06816

Visit Franklin Watts on the internet at:
http://publishing.grolier.com

Catalog details are available from the Library of Congress
Cataloging-in-Publication Data

ISBN 0-531-14549-2 (lib.bdg) 0-531-15446-7 (pbk)

GROLIER
PUBLISHING

Contents

Bridging the Gap

How can you cross a river without getting your feet wet? When human beings realized that bridges were the answer, they used fallen tree trunks.

When cutting tools were invented, they were used to fell the trees and level the wood into planks. Later, bridges were built of stone and metal. In more modern times, bridges have been built across roads, railway lines, canals, and other stretches of water.

▲ This bridge across New River Sound in Florida is raised and lowered many times a day to allow tall-masted boats to pass under it.

Did You Know...

The longest bridge in the world also has a long name! The Second Lake Pontchartrain Causeway in Louisiana was finished in 1969. It is 23.8 miles (38.42 km) long. From the middle of this bridge, you can't see land at all!

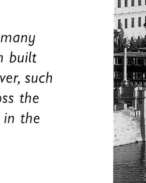

▶ In busy cities, many bridges are often built over the same river, such as these that cross the Vitava in Prague in the Czech Republic.

Bridges Across the Years

tree-trunk bridge

clapper bridge

medieval bridge

iron arch bridge

Bridging Words

Many different words are used in this book to describe bridges and their uses. Can you find the ones below and discover what they mean?

span   cantilever
bascule   suspension
aqueduct   cable-stayed
settlement   clapper bridge

▶ *These houses in Malaysia are built on stilts at the water's edge. Wooden bridges are the only way to cross from one to another.*

bascule bridge   cantilever bridge   suspension bridge

Sticks and Stones

Early types of bridges had drawbacks. Trees that had fallen naturally over streams meant that people could only cross at that place.

Later, people realized that two trunks would be easier to walk across. Even so, bridges like this were difficult for horses and other animals to cross. These bridges could not cross distances greater than the height of a tree, and they were slippery in wet weather.

▲ *This simple style of stone bridge in Devon, England, is called a clapper bridge.*

▲ *A suspended bridge of rope and wood stretches hundreds of feet in the Philippines.*

Early Bridges

In tropical rain forests, vines and creepers hanging from almost every tree could be twisted together to make rope bridges. Although they could span quite long distances, these bridges were difficult to cross because they move and swing.

Bridges made of slabs of stone were much stronger and easier to cross. By putting a supporting stone in the middle, longer distances could be crossed. But huge stones like this are very hard to move and position.

Roman Arches

The Romans realized that arches could be used to build long, strong bridges. An arch spreads the weight of the bridge and anything crossing it over the length of its span. Arches are built of small stones or bricks, which are light and easy to handle. The Romans figured out that lots of arches put together could cross enormous distances.

▶ *The Romans built this beautiful bridge in Spain. It is designed to carry water and is called an aqueduct.*

Try This! A Show of Strength

YOU WILL NEED:

- **4 sturdy books**
- **2 pieces of thin cardboard**
- **2 small containers**
- **20 marbles**

YOU CAN TRY THIS!

You can prove that an arch is a much stronger structure than a flat span.

1 *Arrange two piles of books as shown and place a piece of thin cardboard across them to form a bridge. Place a small container on top and keep adding marbles to it until the bridge bends and collapses. Count the number of marbles you have used.*

2 Bend the second piece of cardboard between two more piles of books as in the picture and place the piece of cardboard across the top. Place the second container on top and add marbles as before.

? How many marbles can the bridge support now? Compare the numbers to see which is the stronger bridge!

Travel and Trade

As people became more skilled at building bridges, roads were built in places where they could not have been built before. Travel and trade increased, and bridges became important areas of business for travelers who met at these crossings.

Stores were even built on bridges. Old London Bridge, built in the twelfth century, was the only bridge across the River Thames until 1750. It was lined with stores and houses several stories high.

◆ The Ponte Vecchio over the River Arno in Florence, Italy, still has stores on it, especially jewelry stores. Stores on bridges are safer from robbery, as a thief does not have many escape routes after his crime.

Rialto Bridge

The Italian city of Venice has hundreds of bridges. They were important to trade. In Shakespeare's play *The Merchant of Venice*, the moneylender, Shylock, talks to one of his clients about doing business on the Rialto Bridge.

Signor Antonio, many a time and oft
In the Rialto you have rated [scolded] me
About my moneys and my usances
[moneylending].
You come to me, and you say,
'Shylock, we would have moneys.'
WILLIAM SHAKESPEARE

Did You Know...

The covered bridges seen throughout New England were based on the drawings of Antonio Palladio, an Italian architect who lived in the 16th century. Often these bridges replaced existing ferry crossings. Over 10,000 were built, but only about 1,000 remain. Most are in Pennsylvania.

Musical Bridges

Bridges became an important part of people's lives, and songs and poems were written about them. This French song is about dancing on the bridge in the southern city of Avignon. It is a round, which means that different voices sing different parts of it at the same time. Divide into four groups. When the first group finishes singing the first line of the verse, the second group starts from the beginning, and so on until all of you are taking part.

Sur le pont d'Avignon,
On y danse, on y danse,
Sur le pont d'Avignon,
On y danse, tout en rond.

On the bridge of Avignon,
Everyone dances, everyone dances,
On the bridge of Avignon,
Everyone dances round and round.

Cities of Bridges

Many places around the world have waterways instead of streets between the houses. People have to cross from one side to the other over a bridge. In Europe, the older parts of Venice in Italy, Amsterdam in the Netherlands, and Hamburg in Germany are built on canals. In some coastal areas of the Far East, where much of the land is swampy, travel by water is often easier than by road.

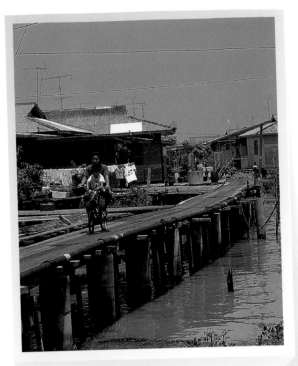

▶ In this part of Malaysia, houses and bridges are raised high on stilts to prevent flooding when the water rises.

Bridges as Landmarks

You may be used to giving people directions by road, but can you do it using waterways? In the old part of Venice, which is built entirely on canals, people find their way through the city via canals rather than roads. Imagine you are in Venice and you have to navigate by canals and bridges. Bridges have become important as landmarks to help travelers find their way.

◀ In medieval times and later, the wealth of the Netherlands was built on trade. Canals like this one in Alkmaar made moving goods easier, but bridges needed to be provided for pedestrians.

Try This!

Look at the map of Venice below. You are starting in a boat beside the Rialto Bridge.

1 Travel south down the Grand Canal when you see Rio di S Salvador on your left, turn into it.

2 Pass under two bridges and take the left fork. Turn right into the Rio San Zulian, pass under four bridges and turn right into the Rio dell Palazzo. Follow it under the Ponte della Paglia. Where are you?

3 Now try it with some friends. Can they follow your directions to another part of the city?

☝ The Bridge of Sighs in Venice got its name from the sounds made by prisoners as they were taken across it to the prison.

Rialto Bridge

Rio della Fava

Grand Canal

Rio di S Salvador

Rio di San Zulian

Rio di San Luca

Rio Fuseri

Rio del Barcaroli

Rio delle Procuratie

Rio del Palazzo

Rio di Sant'Angelo

Rio della Verona

Piazza San Marco

Ponte della Paglia

Rio dell'Albero

Rio San Moise

Canale di San Marco

Bridges of the Mind

Have you noticed that places can look completely different when viewed from a bridge?

The English poet William Wordsworth found that he saw London differently when standing on one of the bridges crossing the river Thames. He was neither in the busy streets nor on the river, but somewhere between these worlds. He explains how he looks afresh at a place he knew well in his poem "Composed on Westminster Bridge, 1802."

Try This!

Can you find other stories and poems in which bridges divide or link people and places, or form a place for something important to happen? If not, why not try writing your own?

YOU CAN TRY THIS!

Earth has not anything to show more fair:
Dull would he be of soul who could pass by
A sight so touching in its majesty:
This City now doth, like a garment, wear
The beauty of the morning; silent, bare,
Ships, towers, domes, theatres, and temples lie
Open unto the fields, and to the sky;
All bright and glittering in the smokeless air.
Never did sun more beautifully steep
In his first splendour, valley, rock, or hill;
Ne'er saw I, never felt, a calm so deep!
The river glideth at his own sweet will:
Dear God! The very houses seem asleep;
And all that mighty heart is lying still!

WILLIAM WORDSWORTH

APPLES OVER A RAINBOW BRIDGE

Many cultures have stories about a bridge that enables gods or people to cross between earth and heaven. Some stories, such as this one from Norse mythology, imagine that a rainbow is a bridge between heaven and earth.

In Asgard, the home of the gods, there was a tree bearing golden apples. Eating them made the gods immortal. The apple tree was looked after by a goddess called Idun. One day, the gods Odin, Honir and Loki crossed a rainbow bridge that led to the human world. When they felt hungry, they killed an ox and made a fire, but the meat would not cook!

"Someone is casting a spell on us," said Odin. "Yes," croaked a voice from above. "It is I."

Looking up, the gods saw a huge eagle. Loki angrily struck the bird with his staff. To his horror, the staff stuck to the bird and his hand. The eagle began to drag Loki along, squawking, "I will let you go if you bring me Idun and her golden apples."

Desperate to escape, Loki brought Idun to the eagle. Suddenly, he realized that the eagle was really the giant Thjazi in disguise. As Thjazi carried Idun off to his fortress, the gods began to age quickly — they needed Idun's apples!

Odin's wife Freya turned Loki into a falcon so he could fly into the giant's fortress and rescue Idun while Thjazi was hunting. On finding Idun, Loki changed her into a nut.

Clutching the nut in his claws, he flew out of the fortress — just as Thjazi came back! Changing into an eagle once more, the angry giant chased Loki right through the human world. The falcon was about to fly over the rainbow bridge to the safety of Asgard when he felt the eagle snapping at his heels. Would he save Idun in time?

Meanwhile Odin had ordered a huge fire to be built in Asgard. As Loki and his precious cargo soared over it, the eagle flew straight into the flames and was destroyed for ever. Loki dropped the nut from his claw and it changed back into Idun. As they ate her golden fruit, the gods became young once more.

A Revolution in Bridges

In the second half of the eighteenth century, factories took the place of workshops. Goods could be made cheaply and on a huge scale. This change was called the Industrial Revolution.

It began in the midlands of England, where there was iron ore to make iron and steel, and coal to heat the furnaces that powered steam engines in the factories. Iron and steel could now be shaped mechanically and used in new ways. One of these was bridge building.

◆ *The first iron bridge was finished in 1779. Iron Bridge at Coalbrookdale in England is still standing today.*

Bridges for the Iron Road

As the Industrial Revolution developed, steam engines were designed as a means of transport, and the first locomotive ran on rails in 1829. Soon, railways were being constructed all over the world, and thousands of bridges needed to be built for them.

◆ *Railways played an important part in the settlement of America. Tracks often had to be built on difficult terrain such as Canyon Diabolo in Arizona.*

The Iron Age

The great age of iron bridges was the second half of the nineteenth century. Many of these bridges were very ornate and were painted in magnificent colors.

◀ *This bridge was built by Isambard Kingdom Brunel, one of the pioneers of engineering on a large scale in iron.*

➡ *The Forth Rail Bridge is 8,244 feet (2,513 meters).*

Try This! A Coat of Paint

YOU WILL NEED:

- **Two iron nails (not galvanized)**
- **Enamel paint or nail varnish**
- **Paintbrush**
- **A saucer or other small tray**
- **Some cotton batting**
- **A small amount of water**

Iron bridges need to be painted frequently. This is because, if not protected, the metal reacts with the air to form rust. This experiment will show you how important that coat of paint is!

1 *Paint one iron nail all over with the enamel paint or nail varnish and allow to dry.*

2 *Put the cotton batting on the saucer and pour enough water on to make the cotton damp.*

3 *Place the painted nail and the unpainted one side by side — but not touching — on the damp cotton. Leave it for a week or two, adding small amounts of water to make sure the cotton is always damp.*

? **What has happened to the nails? Can you see any difference?**

The dark stains on the unpainted nail and cotton are rust, formed when the iron reacts with oxygen in the air to make a substance called iron oxide. If left long enough, the whole nail would turn to rust, and then it would fall apart.

The painted nail, however, should be exactly as you painted it — and rust free!

Raising the Road

The increase in trade worldwide meant that bigger ships were needed to carry the goods. But these could not pass under fixed bridges unless the banks of the river were high enough for the bridge to allow them headroom. The invention of the steam engine meant that bridge builders could use these to lift the deck of the bridge. These bridges are called movable or bascule bridges, meaning that they have two giant "leaves" or bascules that open to allow shipping to pass through.

The stone towers of Tower Bridge are just an attractive skin over a huge iron construction holding it all together.

Did You Know...

Some bascule bridges seem to open much wider than they need to for modern shipping. That is because a hundred years ago there were still sailing ships, and their sails were much wider than the ship underneath.

Bascule means "see-saw" in French.

The bascules are opened by hydraulics — water pumped under pressure. To stop the water from freezing in winter and jamming the bridge, a second set of pipes containing hot water runs next to the hydraulic pipes to warm them.

▶ Tower Bridge in London is a bascule bridge that was built in 1894.

Bridges in Battle

Bridges have played an important part in warfare. By controlling a bridge, an army could prevent the enemy from crossing into the land beyond.

Horatius Holds the Bridge

This poem tells of a battle of ancient Rome, in which Horatius defends a bridge to save the city from the enemy army. In this extract, the leaders of Rome have decided that the bridge must be destroyed. Horatius and fellow soldiers agree to cross the bridge and hold the enemy back, to give the Romans time to destroy it.

But meanwhile axe and lever
Have manfully been plied;
And now the bridge hangs tottering
Above the boiling tide.
"Come back, come back, Horatius!"
Loud cried the Fathers all.
"Back, Lartius! Back, Herminius!
Back, ere the ruin fall!"

Back darted Spurius Lartius;
Herminius darted back:
And, as they passed, beneath their feet
They felt the timbers crack.
But, when they turned their faces,
And on the farther shore
Saw brave Horatius stand alone,
They would have crossed once more.

But with a crash like thunder
Fell every loosened beam,
And, like a dam, the mighty wreck
Lay right athwart the stream!
LORD MACAULAY

Moving Bridges

Destroying a bridge in order to defend a city could be very effective, but it also meant that after the battle, another one had to be built to restore access to the other side of the river. This took time and could be costly, so engineers devised ways of building bridges that could be withdrawn and then restored when danger had passed.

Drawbridges

In the Middle Ages, lords made their own protective waterways by digging moats around their castles. The bridges across them could be raised and lowered, just like bascule bridges today.

Did You Know...

Soldiers crossing bridges have to break step so that they are not marching in time. If they do march in time, the vibrations set up by their feet can cause the bridge to collapse.

Temporary Bridges

An army faced with a stretch of water and no way to cross it needs to be able to build a bridge very quickly. A Bailey bridge, named after its inventor, Sir D. Bailey, is one solution. It is made of lattice steel parts that can be put together at high speed. Another method is to make a floating bridge by lashing boats together.

◀ *A lattice of steel is very strong. Even a quickly built Bailey bridge, like this one in Cambodia, can support heavy traffic.*

Water Over the Bridge

It is not only people and vehicles that can use bridges. Since Roman times, water has also flowed across bridges. These kinds of bridges are called aqueducts, but why were they necessary?

Aqueducts

Water always flows to the lowest point. If water was piped down a valley, it would stay at the bottom and not climb up the other side unless a pump was used. By taking the water across a high aqueduct, it remains at the same level and can continue to flow.

Try This!

Take a length of clear plastic hose and hold both ends in one hand. Using a funnel, pour some water into the hose. Notice how the water on both sides always reaches the same level. What happens if you raise one end of the tube?

Try This!

Bridges are so important that, over many years, lots of expressions about them have entered our language. Do you know what these mean?

- burning your bridges
- water under the bridge
- we'll cross that bridge when we come to it

Can you think of any more?

◀ *The Dundas aqueduct, near Bath, England, enables the canal to cross a road.*

Number Work

A canal bridge has to be very, very strong to support the weight of the water it carries. A cubic foot of water weighs 2,000 pounds. How much water would a section of canal 10 feet long, 10 feet wide and 2 feet deep contain and what would it weigh?

◀ *The Pont du Gard aqueduct in France was built by the Romans. It is used to transport water across water.*

The Age of Canals

By using locks, canals solve the problem of water always flowing toward the lowest point.

In the eighteenth century, engineers built networks of canals all over Europe to carry the mass-produced goods being made in the new factories. These were loaded onto horse-drawn barges. This was the quickest form of transport before railways were built.

Hanging by Wires

Traditionally, bridges were held up from underneath by the river banks, by piers built up from the riverbed, or by arches. By the beginning of the nineteenth century, engineers such as Thomas Telford from Scotland were designing bridges whose weight was supported from above by wires. These were called suspension bridges.

Suspension Bridges

In a suspension bridge, the road or railway really does hang from hundreds of steel cables. The tops of these are attached to two enormous cables slung between high towers that are positioned opposite each other on each side of the river. Modern suspension bridges have the advantage of being able to span huge distances.

The massive cables are made from hundreds of wires no thicker than a pencil. They are bound together with galvanized wire that will not rust.

The cables are anchored in concrete on the riverbanks. These counterbalance the weight of the bridge and its traffic.

The towers are slightly farther apart at the top than at the bottom because the surface of the Earth is curved. Hold two pencils on a ball and you will see why.

The platform that supports the road or railway is called the deck. This is made from steel.

Deep foundations for the towers reach down to firm clay or rock under the riverbed.

Collapsing Bridges

Suspension bridges that span huge distances have to be strong enough to withstand fierce side winds. The Tacoma Narrows Bridge (pictured right) in Washington State was unable to withstand such winds and was therefore a spectacular failure. "Galloping Gertie" — so-called because the roadway moved up and down like a roller coaster — collapsed on November 7, 1940.

Try This! Build Your Own Suspension Bridge

YOU WILL NEED:

- 2 empty cereal boxes of the same size
- ruler
- scissors
- stiff cardboard
- tape
- glue
- string

1 Cut rectangles of the same size right through both boxes. They need to be slightly wider than your road.

2 Glue the boxes about 28 inches (70 cm) apart on a thick piece of cardboard.

3 Twist together lengths of string to make a thicker rope. The string needs to be long enough to stretch from the edge of the base, up and over the two boxes, and down to the base again. Tape your ropes to the base. Don't pull them too tight.

4 Cut a roadway from thick cardboard and position it through the boxes.

5 Loop string under the road and tie it to the ropes on both sides, so that the road is suspended from the ropes.

Cable-Stayed Bridges

Another way of supporting a bridge by wires is to have hundreds of narrow cables stretching from the tops of two or more towers down to each side of the roadway. As each cable reaches farther and farther along the deck to support it, a splendid fan effect is created.

➤ *The Ting Kau Bridge crossing to Tsing Yi Island, Hong Kong, is an elegant example of a cable-stayed bridge.*

Try This! Wires and Weight

Are several wires or threads tied together really stronger than one?

You can find out by tying a thread to the handle of a basket or bag. Hold the bag by the thread and add more and more weight to the bag. Record the weight at which the thread breaks.

Now do the same experiment with two threads. Does it make any difference if they are twisted together?

Make a graph to show the strength of one, two, three, and more threads. Can you predict, from your findings, how much weight six threads could hold?

Beautiful Bridges

→ Bridges that cross water often create beautiful reflections. When designing a bridge, it is important to think about how it will look from all aspects. In this case, the underside of the Ha'penny Bridge, Dublin, Ireland, is mirrored by the water running beneath it.

▲ The modern Caltrava Footbridge in Bilbao, Spain, is as beautiful as it is useful.

Bridges are built purely to solve the problem of crossing open spaces or water, but many of their designs are very beautiful, too.

Design a bridge yourself that will be both useful and beautiful. It will help to imagine where your bridge will be positioned. A busy harbor and a village stream, for example, would need very different bridges.

Natural Bridges

Human beings have built many kinds of bridges, but some have been built by nature over many thousands of years. Rock bridges such as this one, found in a desert in Utah, have been formed by wind and rain wearing away the solid rock from underneath.

Land Bridges

Millions of years ago, the world's continents were joined together by land bridges to form one great landmass called Pangaea.

The dinosaurs were able to cross these bridges, which is why fossil remains of the same species have been found in countries on different sides of the world.

◀ *In this picture, continental drift has caused many of the landmasses on Earth to join together at various points.*

When People Wandered

More than 20,000 years ago, there was an ice age that lasted hundreds of years. Much of the world's land was covered in a vast sheet of ice. An ice bridge formed between Asia and the American continent. When herds of game animals began to drift over the ice bridge, people followed in order to continue hunting the animals for food. These were the first people in America. Some of them stayed in the north, but others, over thousands of years, kept on walking — right down to the tip of South America.

Europeans, too, traveled over land bridges and settled in lands that are now islands. The very early inhabitants of the British Isles, for example, crossed over from Europe about 7,000 years ago.

Number Work

The vast areas of ocean on our planet make some parts of the world seem farther away than they really are. What if in the future a bridge was built across the Atlantic Ocean? It would need to be at least 3,000 miles (4,800 km) long. If a car could travel along it at 70 miles (113 km) per hour, how long would it take to make the trip?

What's More...

London Bridge Is Falling Down

You may have heard this rhyme about the collapse of this famous bridge.

London Bridge is falling down,
Falling down, falling down,
London Bridge is falling down,
My fair lady.

Some say this rhyme refers to a wooden bridge across the Thames, dating from Roman times, which Norwegian Vikings attacked in 1014. Others think it dates from the eighteenth century, when Old London Bridge, built 600 years before, began to crumble. The "fair lady" is the queen of the time.

Did You Know...

In 1831, a new London Bridge was built to replace the old one that was crumbling. But it only lasted just over 130 years. Then it was taken down, piece by piece, and shipped across the Atlantic. It was rebuilt in Lake Havasu City, Arizona, as a tourist attraction.

◀ *This version of London Bridge did not fall down. It was dismantled stone by stone and rebuilt in the United States.*

Look! No Nails!

Most bridges would fall apart without the thousands of nails, screws, and rivets that hold them together. This wooden bridge in Cambridge, England, however, was originally put together with no nails at all. It is called the Mathematical Bridge, probably because the designer used pages of plans to come up with such an extraordinary idea. The story goes that when it had to be taken apart for repairs, no one could figure out how to put it together again, and nails had to be used.

▲ *The Mathematical Bridge spans the River Cam in Cambridge.*

The Shape of Bridges to Come?

Bridges that do not carry very heavy loads do not have to be made out of tough materials like iron, steel, and concrete. This indoor bridge in the London Science Museum is made of glass! It can carry the weight of a crowd of people, but what do you think is holding it up? It seems as though it is floating in mid-air, but if you look closely, you can see hundreds of fine steel cables only a fraction of an inch thick that are keeping it from crashing down to the floor below.

Glossary

aqueduct: a bridge for carrying water across valleys or low ground.

Bailey bridge: a temporary bridge made of steel parts that can be quickly put together. Bailey bridges were invented by Sir D. Bailey.

barge: a long, narrow boat designed to carry heavy goods along canals.

bascule bridge: a bridge with a roadway that can be raised to allow ships to pass underneath.

cable-stayed bridge: a bridge in which the road or railway is supported by wires suspended from single pillars.

canal: a specially dug waterway for transporting people and goods by boat.

cantilever: a long beam or part of a bridge fixed at only one end.

clapper bridge: an early bridge made of slabs of stone supported by large stones or stacks of stones.

deck: the platform of a suspension bridge that holds the road or railway.

foundations: strong supports, usually buried underground, to take the weight of a building or bridge.

furnace: a very hot fire in which metal can be melted.

galvanize: to coat iron with zinc so that it does not rust.

hydraulic: powered by the movement of liquid in pipes.

Industrial Revolution: a period from the late eighteenth to the early nineteenth century when machines and methods of manufacturing things developed very quickly. Factories made it possible to make things faster and in larger numbers than ever before.

iron ore: the raw material from which iron is made.

landmark: a building, hill, bridge, or other feature that stands out in the landscape and helps travelers find their way.

Answers

p.11 on the Canal di San Marco.

p.19 400,000 pounds

p.27 around 42 hours.

Glossary

lattice: a criss-cross pattern.

lock: a pair of gates across a canal that allows boats to go down or up slopes. The boat floats between the gates while the water level rises or falls to match the stretch of canal ahead.

Middle Ages: a period in history, from around A.D. 1000 to A.D. 1500.

moneylender: someone who lends money, usually asking for extra money (interest) when it is repaid.

navigate: to find the way when traveling.

Pangaea: the name given by scientists to the great landmass that existed on Earth before separate continents broke away to form the shapes we know today.

rain forest: tropical forest with heavy rainfall, providing a habitat for a huge number of plants and animals.

round: a song in which different voices can sing a different part of the song at the same time, one starting after the other.

settlement: a place where people have made their homes.

span: the distance that a bridge has to cross.

steel: an alloy (mixture) of iron and carbon that is very strong.

story: one floor or level of a building.

suspension bridge: a bridge in which the road or railway is suspended from wires attached to pairs of tall pillars.

trade: buying and selling things.

vibrations: tiny rhythmic movements.

waterway: a stretch of water, such as a canal or river, along which people can travel or transport goods in boats.

workshops: places where goods are made by small groups of people, usually by hand.

Index